# REFLECTIONS
## OF IOWA STATE

Published by the
Iowa State University Alumni Association

Published by the Iowa State University Alumni Association,
Jeffery W. Johnson, president and publisher

Written, edited, and designed by Karol Crosbie, '72, '84

Art direction and production by Carole Gieseke

Production assistance by Karen Knight

Printed by Tru Art Color Graphics, Iowa City, Iowa

ISBN 0-9704094-0-0

Iowa State University Alumni Association / Fisher-Nickell Hall /
214 Richardson Court / Ames, Iowa 50011-1307

## PHOTOGRAPHERS

Todd Asmus*
Erin Axtell, '97
Laurence Burkhalter
Lou Cathcart*
George Christensen
Anthony Connor
Jim Fosse, ISU Veterinary
    Biomedical Communications
Jean Harkin
Louise Haug
Jim Heemstra
Josh Herrington

ISU Photo Service
    Bob Elbert
    Michael Haynes
Barb Kashian
Kapil Khanna*
Pete Krumhardt, '74
Mary Richards, '75
Jon Rusho, '96
Mark Schuelke
Dorcas Speer
Elizabeth Stanley
Jim Wilcox, '80, '98
Don Wishart, '62, '69

*Current ISU student

## PHOTO CONTRIBUTORS

Farm House Museum Collection,
    ISU Museums
ISU Library / University Archives
Diane Nelson, '72, '89
VISIONS Magazine

JIM HEEMSTRA

GEORGE CHRISTENSEN

No matter how beautiful a new surrounding is, it takes awhile before it feels like home. I remember when my wife, Ellen, and my two daughters and I first moved into the Knoll in 1965. It was gracious and stately, but when night came we couldn't get over the noise! There was the hum of traffic from busy Lincoln Way and the shouts of students from nearby Welch Hall. And the bells! That Campanile chimed all night.

Whether it's a lonely freshman kept awake by the strange sounds of a new dormitory room, or a university president tolled awake by chimes, this place called Iowa State has watched over old and young Iowa Staters for more than 132 years. I love the impressions of one of our earliest alums, as she approached Iowa State College for the first time. *History of Reminisces of Iowa Agricultural College* records the memories of Winifred Dudley Shaw, who graduated in 1897. Winifred was 10 years old, and Iowa State was in its infancy – a prairie, a farm, a cattle barn, and the unfinished Farm House, where Winifred would live with her stepfather, Adonijah Strong Welch, Iowa State's first president.

Winifred recalls her childhood impressions, as her family's wagon pulled up to the Farm House in September of 1868:

*"I think I can recall every article of furniture in that house. A long office table with heavy wooden chairs around it, a dirty inkstand and some disreputable-*

*looking pens, a newspaper or two and some state reports, a great rusty iron soft coal stove, two cases of books, and a big thermometer. The floor was bare save for the muddy tracks of workmen's boots, and the air was heavy with stale tobacco smoke."*

But like the generations that would come after her, Iowa State soon became a home for young Winifred. Her stepfather planted trees and flowers, and more buildings joined the Farm House. By the time Winifred graduated in 1897, the prairie had given way to more than 45 buildings, including greenhouses, dormitories, barns, faculty lodgings, and the beginning of the first botanical garden. Morrill Hall and Agricultural Hall (today's Catt Hall) were sparkling new. In fact, the 1897 equivalent of today's admissions catalog boasts that "the true principles of landscape gardening have been so faithfully observed in the gardening, and in the location of buildings and drives, as to make of the entire campus a large and beautiful park."

A little more than 100 years later, the nation's leading landscape architects would come to the same conclusion. Our campus *does* look like a park! In 1999, the American Society of Landscape Architects designated it as a "medallion site," and one of the most beautiful in the country.

But it takes more than a park to feel at home. True connections come from shared experiences with other Iowa Staters. As I recall the many faces that made up my Iowa State experience, I am proud of the vision of the people who came before me, who believed that a college education should be available to all people – to the daughters of farmers and to the sons of laborers. Justin Smith Morrill's Land Grant Act was the empowerment of this vision, and Iowa State College was its first embodiment.

If the institution of Iowa State University is the sum of all that has gone before us, so are we, as individuals, the sum of our memories. Mine are extraordinarily pleasant. My family soon made the Knoll our home, and in the years that followed, our love for Iowa State continued to grow. I remember both the small places and the big ones – the imposing steps of Beardshear that I climbed at least once a day; the secluded, peaceful little stone bench beside the Campanile; our wide, welcoming central campus; and the small bridge, overhung with green, that spans College Creek behind the Knoll.

May this book help to refresh old memories and build new connections.

*W. Robert Parks*
ISU President Emeritus, 1965-1986

JIM HEEMSTRA

JIM HEEMSTRA

## A LAND-GRANT LEGACY

Morrill Hall, built in 1890, was named after Justin Smith Morrill, a U.S. Representative from Vermont. Morrill introduced the Land Grant Act, which granted public lands for educational institutions. Iowa State was the first designated land-grant institution.

One of the first buildings on campus, Morrill Hall initially housed a library and museum. It was also used as a chapel and contained zoology, entomology, and geology laboratories. For a short time, it even sported a barber shop in the basement.

LAURENCE BURKHALTER

*"At this time (1890) the beautiful building which was named for its provider, was erected and the library was moved to Morrill Hall, where a most pleasant reading room was in waiting – new books, shelves, and handsome rugs for the floors make the place very inviting, and hundreds of students visit the library daily."*

– HISTORY OF REMINISCES OF IOWA AGRICULTURAL COLLEGE

*The Campanile, circa 1904-1907.*

## THE CAMPANILE

*"Another improvement which will grace our campus ... will be the new bell tower and chime of bells. The bells will be the gift of Professor Stanton, to the college in memory of his wife, Mrs. Margaret McDonald Stanton. The bells will be set to music, and their rich, mellow tones will be heard miles away."*

– L. MAE FELLOWS, CLASS OF 1897

PHOTOS BY JIM HEEMSTRA

*Above: Over the years, the Campanile has frequently been the site of student proclamations and living experiments.*

*"And soften down the rugged road of life."*

– INSCRIPTION ON ONE OF THE
ORIGINAL 10 BELLS OF THE CAMPANILE

JIM HEEMSTRA

DON WISHART

MARK SCHUELKE

*Above: ISU carillonneur, Tin-Shi Tam.*

*Left: One of Iowa State's oldest traditions is that of being "campaniled." Once you are kissed under the Campanile at midnight, the tradition goes, you are officially a coed.*

ISU ARCHIVES

## THE HUB

Since 1892, the Hub has been a student center of activity – first as a waiting room for the Ames and College Railway, then as a bookstore, post office, and the perfect place to hold a pep rally. It later became a ticket office and copy center.

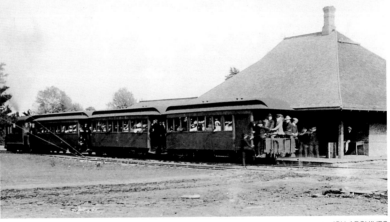

ISU ARCHIVES

ISU ARCHIVES

ISU ARCHIVES

*The Hub through the decades: Circa 1900 (facing page, top and center), 1910 (facing page, bottom), 1960s (left) and 1990s (below).*

JIM HEEMSTRA

## THE FOUNTAIN OF THE FOUR SEASONS

Sculpted by Christian Petersen, the Fountain of the Four Seasons
has been an Iowa State landmark since 1941, a gift of the 1936
Veishea Central Committee. The maidens disappeared from campus
in the spring of 1996 for major conservation, and reappeared in
1998, gleaming and ready to face another 50 years.

PHOTOS BY JIM HEEMSTRA

*Styles have changed, but Curtiss Hall remains the same, as illustrated by these nearly identical photos taken around 1910 and 1965.*

## CURTISS HALL

First named Agriculture Hall, Curtiss Hall was built in 1909. Its name was changed to Curtiss Hall in 1944 to honor Dean of Agriculture Charles F. Curtiss.

ISU PHOTO SERVICE

ANTHONY CONNOR

*April 1995: In the midst of Veishea frivolity, the flag is flying at half-mast to mourn the victims of the Oklahoma City bombing, which had occurred just days before.*

JIM HEEMSTRA

ISU PHOTO SERVICE

*St. Patrick's Day parade, circa 1915.*

ISU ARCHIVES

JIM HEEMSTRA

DORCAS SPEER

## BEARDSHEAR HALL

Beardshear Hall's namesake, William Miller Beardshear, who presided from 1891-1902, was one of Iowa State's most popular presidents.

*"President Beardshear . . appeared to have a special sense whereby he could find out what was going on. How did he find out? How did he know that it was a certain student in the group before him that stole the farmers' chickens?"*

– JOHN HUNGERFORD, CLASS OF 1877

*Beardshear Hall serves students on many levels.*

LAURENCE BURKHALTER

## OLD MUSIC HALL

Old Music Hall was first built as a home for one of the college's original faculty, and then occupied by Dean Stanton. It was used to house the first college tea-room and later became the first Domestic Technology Building; finally, it was turned over to the Music Department.

The old structure was razed in 1978 to make way for today's Music Hall.

DORCAS SPEER

ISU ARCHIVES

ISU ARCHIVES

ISU ARCHIVES

JIM HEEMSTRA

*Top: Looking across the lake to the old Veterinary Hospital where the Memorial Union now stands, 1918.*

*Left and center: Improvements were made to the lake in 1933.*

*Above: Rowing on Lake LaVerne, 1999.*

28

MARY RICHARDS

## LAKE LAVERNE

In 1916, LaVerne Noyes, class of 1872, a wealthy Chicago
manufacturer, donated $10,000 for landscaping the campus
and for constructing the lake that bears his name.

*"If agreeable to you, I shall be glad to bear the expense of
constructing a lake at the Iowa State College Grounds in the
valley south of Dean Stanton's house."*

– A JUNE 15, 1915, LETTER FROM LAVERNE NOYES
TO THE BOARD OF EDUCATION

LOU CATHCART

## LANCELOT AND ELAINE

Lancelot and Elaine first arrived on campus in 1935 when they were launched from a swan-shaped barge, a gift of the Veishea Central Committee. Although the swans have changed, their names remain the same. They will always be Lancelot and Elaine.

JIM HEEMSTRA

LAURENCE BURKHALTER

JIM HEEMSTRA

JIM HEEMSTRA

## SWAN AGAIN, OFF AGAIN

In an effort to support the Iowa Department of Natural Resources' goal to propagate trumpeter swans, which are native to Iowa, the university introduced the first trumpeters to Lake LaVerne in 1996. But after four years, not only had the pair produced no babies, they had gained the reputation for irascible dispositions and a wanderlust that sent them marching everywhere, including across Lincoln Way.

They were replaced in November of 1999 with a silent pair who were expected to honor their historic heritage and stay put in the lake. They proved just as rambunctious as their trumpeting predecessors. Lake LaVerne was swanless during the winter of 1999-2000, as the university prepared once again to find the perfect pair. Today, the perfect pair once again reigns.

*The wooden bridge near the Memorial Union (shown above in 1935) has become a bygone memory.*

## THE MEMORIAL UNION

In the 1920s, a group of students came up with a great idea: to combine two Iowa State needs – a building for social events and activities and a World War I memorial. All the money for the building was raised privately, and the Memorial Union was established as a private, not-for-profit corporation, a status that continues today.

JIM HEEMSTRA

JIM HEEMSTRA

Children and students used to stand on "Wishing Well Bridge" to toss pennies into College Creek. Although its magical properties are no longer an active part of ISU folklore, the bridge that spans the creek between the Knoll and Memorial Union is still a well-used spot.

JIM HEEMSTRA

MICHAEL HAYNES

## THE ART OF CHRISTIAN PETERSEN

Christian Petersen was invited to become Iowa State's first (and only) sculptor-in-residence in 1934. From his studio in the Veterinary Quadrangle, for the next 21 years, Petersen created works that would become beloved campus icons.

*Facing page: The Marriage Ring, south of MacKay Hall.*

*This page: Dairy panel and detail in the courtyard of today's Food Sciences Building.*

PHOTOS BY JIM HEEMSTRA

*Above: The Gentle Doctor and bas relief panel at the College of Veterinary Medicine.*

*Near right: Gentle Doctor detail.*

*Far right: Madonna of the Prairie, in the Lagomarcino courtyard.*

GEORGE CHRISTENSEN

JIM HEEMSTRA

ISU ARCHIVES

MICHAEL HAYNES

*Top: Beardshear can be seen going up to the right of Alumni Hall. The buildings were both constructed around 1904 and shared the same architectural firm, Proudfoot and Bird.*

JIM HEEMSTRA

JIM HEEMSTRA

JIM HEEMSTRA

53

LAURENCE BURKHALTER

*Facing page, top: Students brave a frosty morning.*

*Facing page, bottom: The sculpted figures of William King in "Forward" seem to be busily rushing forward.*

*Above: Students Mark Snyder and Dan Thilo used an evolutionary theme in their Focus sculpture, "Spring Favor," displayed during Veishea, 1977.*

JIM HEEMSTRA

BOB ELBERT

JOSH HERRINGTON

JIM HEEMSTRA

*Facing page, top: One of the muses from the fourth floor parapet of Marston Hall guards a snowy campus.*

*Facing page, bottom: Frosty watches over Marston Hall.*

*Above: Lancelot and Elaine keep guard at Lake LaVerne.*

*Left: A G-Nome atop Molecular Biology watches over the campus at dusk.*

ISU MUSEUMS

*The Knapp family in front of the Farm House, circa 1885. Seaman Knapp (center) was Iowa State's second president.*

## THE FARM HOUSE

Completed in 1865, the Farm House was Iowa State's first building. It provided housing for the farm manager and was home to the college's early faculty, staff, and students. Today, it is a museum.

ISU ARCHIVES

*Charles Curtiss, professor of agriculture, and his family moved to the Farm House in the late 1800s. This photo was taken around 1905.*

*Facing page: Jars line the kitchen windows of the Farm House.*
*Left: Snowy berries festoon Farm House.*

*Above: Agricultural Hall, circa 1900.*

## CATT HALL

Alumni on campus between 1928 and 1995 knew it as Old Botany. Their predecessors knew it as Agricultural Hall. Today it is Catt Hall, named after Carrie Chapman Catt, the only female graduate in Iowa State College's Class of 1880, who founded the League of Women Voters. Built in 1892, Catt Hall is one the oldest buildings on campus. Its strategic central location and spectacular renovation makes it one of Iowa State's architectural jewels.

The renovation of Catt Chapman Catt Hall caught the imagination of thousands of people. More than 3,000 women are honored in the Plaza of Heroines, which stretches in front of the hall (right and facing page, top) and was made possible by donors from across the nation.

The building was dedicated on Oct. 6, 1995. In attendance were ISU President Martin Jischke, Lt. Gov. Joy Corning, and Mary Louise Smith (below right). Also participating were "sufragettes." (below left).

Facing page, bottom: Carrie Chapman Catt's ISU graduation portrait.

PHOTOS BY BARB KASHIAN

JIM HEEMSTRA

*Above: Coeds
studying at the
Armory in the '50s.*

*Right: Studying at
the Parks Library.*

*Left: "Freshman Days" at the Armory, 1954.*

*Below: Relaxing at the Parks Library.*

*Insect Toxocology, 1930*

JIM HEEMSTRA

*Two Iowa State students from different cultures and different times pour over their work.*

## NEW REALITIES

In 1939, an Iowa State alum and professor named John Vincent Atanasoff began work on a revolutionary machine. Frustrated by the time it took to solve algebraic equations, Atanasoff created a machine the size of a small desk, using 300 vacuum tubes, rotating drums, and cards. It would be 58 years before the world fully credited the Iowa State professor with inventing the first digital electronic computer. Today, Iowa State has two of the most sophisticated virtual reality laboratories in the world.

MICHAEL HAYNES

and Handle

CK CLOSE

ISU ARCHIVES

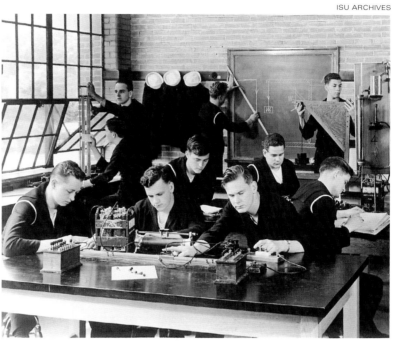

*Far left: C2, ISU's first virtual reality laboratory.*

*Near left: Engineering students in the 1940s.*

*Below left: The first digital computer was invented at Iowa State by John Vincent Atanasoff (below right).*

ISU ARCHIVES

PETE KRUMHARDT

*"I have always taken the position that there is enough credit for everyone in the invention and development of the electronic computer."*

– JOHN VINCENT ATANASOFF,
M.S. 1926, MATHEMATICS

*A woman scientist in today's world.*

## CURTISS-WRIGHT CADETTES

In 1942, World War II was draining men from the work force at exactly the time that trained engineers were needed to keep factories operating. Curtiss-Wright Airplane Company recruited and paid expenses for 700 young women to receive intensive training that would prepare them to work in airplane factories. Iowa State was one of seven colleges in the United States to participate in the program.

The cadettes lived at the Memorial Union while they were at Iowa State:

*"If you were standing at one end of any of three floors in the upper part of the Memorial Union about six forty-five in the morning, you would be apt to hear a succession of alarm clocks and soon, increasing signs of activity. That would be the beginning of a day with a Curtiss-Wright Cadette."*

– MARJORIE ALLEN, CADETTE
FROM *THE IOWA ENGINEER*, APRIL 1942

ISU ARCHIVES

ISU PHOTO SERVICE

*Above: Lining up for registration in the '50s.*

*Left: Today's students can register for classes online.*

75

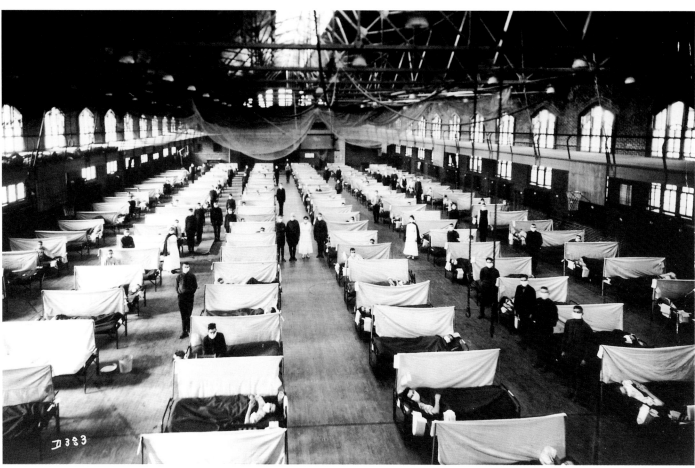

*Above: A Fourth of July picnic around 1900. President Beardshear is the heavily bearded man under the far right window, holding his hat.*

*Facing page: The Spanish Influenza epidemic in 1918 turned the State Gym into a hospital.*

*"All students are in quarantine now for two weeks. We can't leave campus. This is a disappointment to me especially today because I had planned on taking a hike out to North Woods. . . We have three hospitals here now and another one is to be opened soon."*

– FROM THE LETTERS OF ROBERT W. BRECKENRIDGE,
OCTOBER 1918, CLASS OF '32, '34, '38

*Veterinary Quadrangle, 1913*

MICHAEL HAYNES

*Molecular Biology, 1998.*

*Slam dunk, Towers
Residence Halls
basketball court.*

JIM HEEMSTRA

CONTRIBUTED BY DIANE NELSON

*Push ball was a popular sport in the early 1900s. Classes pitted themselves against each other, as they pushed the heavy, sawdust-filled ball from one end zone to another. The game was rowdy and fun-filled, with equal amounts of energy spent pushing the ball, and pulling opponents off of it.*

CONTRIBUTED BY DIANE NELSON

ISU ARCHIVES

IOWA STATE CYCLONES

JIM WILCOX

VISIONS MAGAZINE

83

*Women's volleyball, 1918.*

*"Take care of your health; a feeble body is
like a rickety engine."*

— ANSON MARSTON
FROM *THE IOWA ENGINEER*, OCTOBER 1914

*ISU's first women's soccer team was created in 1996.*

PHOTOS BY JIM HEEMSTRA

PHOTOS BY JIM HEEMSTRA

ISU ARCHIVES

*Baseball, 1932*

## COLLEGE YELL: 1898

*Rah! Rah! Rah!*
*Hoop! Lah! Lee!*
*Hip! Ha! Rip! Rah!*
*I! S! C!*

## ISU FIGHT SONG: TODAY

*Oh we will fight, fight, fight for*
*Iowa State,*
*And may her colors ever fly.*
*Yes we will fight with*
*might for Iowa State,*
*With a will to do or die,*
*Rah! Rah! Rah!*
*Loyal sons forever true,*
*And we will fight the battle through.*
*And when we hit that line we'll hit it hard,*
*Every yard for I.S.U.*

– Jack Barker, '30; Manly Rice,'30; Paul Gnam, '32

90

JIM HEEMSTRA

JIM HEEMSTRA

ISU ARCHIVES

## VEISHEA

The first Veishea was held on May 11-13, 1922, and was named by combining the first letters of the five divisions – Veterinary, Engineering, Industrial Science, Home Economics, and Agriculture.

ISU ARCHIVES

JIM HEEMSTRA

## CHERRY PIES

Iowa State's famous pies first made their appearance in 1921, the year before the first Veishea. The Home Economics Club made 2,000 pies and sold them as part of HEc Day. Today, more than 8,000 pies are produced by a crew of 100 student cooks and organizers.

JIM HEEMSTRA

JIM HEEMSTRA

MICHAEL HAYNES

JIM HEEMSTRA

MICHAEL HAYNES

96

MICHAEL HAYNES

MICHAEL HAYNES

*Cy the Cardinal first made his appearance at Homecoming, 1954. Today, he's everywhere – greeting students, alumni, and friends.*

JIM HEEMSTRA

JIM HEEMSTRA

## THE MAINTENANCE SHOP

Once a greasy workshop for maintenance and repair, the
Maintenance Shop in the basement of the Memorial Union
began serving music and snacks in 1973. The M-Shop soon
acquired the reputation as one of the best venues for jazz and
folk music in the Midwest.

JIM HEEMSTRA

*Top: Campustown has long been a popular destination for Iowa State students. To date, however, no campaniling has been observed at the clock tower on Welch Avenue.*

*Left: From yesteryear, the College Pipe Shop, southwest corner of Lincoln Way and Welch Avenue.*

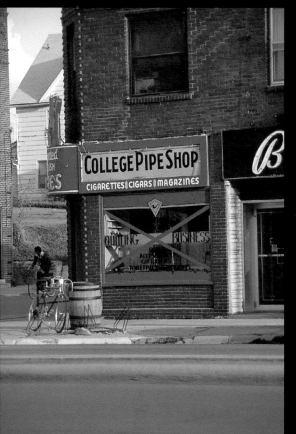

JIM WILCOX

*"I have no words to adequately express my impressions of dear old I.S.C. (Iowa State College). All I am and all I hope to be I owe in a very large measure to this blessed institution."*

– GEORGE WASHINGTON CARVER

PETE KRUMHARDT

JIM HEEMSTRA

JIM HEEMSTRA

ISU ARCHIVES

## GEORGE WASHINGTON CARVER

Above is the graduation photo of George Washington Carver, who received his B.S. from Iowa State in 1894. He went on to receive his M.S. in 1896 and was Iowa State's first African American faculty member.

JIM HEEMSTRA

"One (educational reform of this institution) is the withdrawal of the ancient classics from the place of honor which they have largely held in our college curriculum, and the liberal substitution of those branches of natural science which underlie the industries of this beautiful state. The other is the free admission of young women on equal terms with young men."

– FROM THE INAUGURAL SPEECH OF A.S. WELCH,
IOWA STATE'S SECOND PRESIDENT, MARCH 17, 1869

*Memorial Union, 1963.*

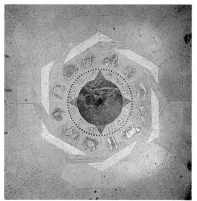

## THE ZODIAC

Who knows what prompted the first student to step over the bronze zodiac relief on the floor of the new Gold Star Hall addition to the Memorial Union in 1938? But ever since that step was taken, students have understood that to step on the zodiac is to ensure that they will flunk their next exam.

MICHAEL HAYNES

JIM HEEMSTRA

MICHAEL HAYNES

MICHAEL HAYNES

JIM HEEMSTRA

*The Towers Residence Halls were built in the early 1960s.*

ISU PHOTO SERVICE

*Above: Spring flowers at Roberts Hall.*

*Below: The trailers, quonset huts, and metal shelters that first made up Pammel Court were purchased for $1 each from the U.S. military to house an explosion of post-World War II students. A village that was supposed to be temporary hung around for the next 50 years. The last unit was torn down in 1998.*

*Facing page: Vietnam protesters wind their way past Lake LaVerne, 1970.*

*This page: Students brave an Iowa winter.*

PETE KRUMHARDT

JON RUSHO

*A skate-boarder keeps precarious balance in his flight over the steps of the Parks Library. Around the corner, "The Left Sided Angel" keeps its own balance.*

JIM HEEMSTRA

*"The ability of the angel to stay upright affirms the ability of human kind to stay in balance."*

– "THE LEFT SIDED ANGEL" SCULPTOR STEPHEN DE STAEBLER

ISU ARCHIVES

*Curators restore the Grant Wood mural, "Breaking the Prairie Sod," at the Parks Library, 1979.*

JIM HEEMSTRA

*An ISU maintenance worker applies his artistry to the Power Plant.*

*Top: Walking past Stephens Auditorium.*

*Above: Hilton Coliseum, constructed in 1964, flooded in 1993.*

*Left: One of the focal points of Stephens Auditorium is its 3,000 pound silk curtain. The curtain was woven in Kyoto, Japan, on the largest continuous loom in the world.*

*Below: Spring at the Iowa State Center.*

115

ISU PHOTO SERVICE

ISU PHOTO SERVICE

ERIN AXTELL

*The changing moods of Stephens Auditorium.*

JIM HEEMSTRA

## CONCERT ON THE GREEN

Music often welcomes back the university family at the beginning of the school year. Here, the Des Moines Symphony plays well after twilight.

JIM HEEMSTRA

117

KAPIL KHANNA

JIM HEEMSTRA

*Top: Branches paint a snowy pattern against the Agronomy Building.*

*Bottom: A storm gathers over the Agronomy Greenhouse.*

JIM HEEMSTRA

GEORGE CHRISTENSEN

*The Marston Water Tower is a daily reminder of yesterday's technology to scientists at the Molecular Biology Building.*

ISU PHOTO SERVICE

Top: ISU's first
horticulture garden
appeared in 1914,
located near the
Agronomy Building.

Bottom: The second
garden was located
across from the
Physical Plant.

Facing page:
Today's Reiman
Gardens are located
not far from Jack
Trice Stadium.

ISU PHOTO SERVICE

JEAN HARKIN

122

*The garden campanile at Reiman Gardens.*

JIM HEEMSTRA

JIM HEEMSTRA

PHOTOS BY JIM HEEMSTRA

## FESTIVAL OF LIGHTS

The tradition of lighting the large pine on central campus for Christmas began in 1914. Today, the Festival of Lights includes hundreds of luminaries, the celebration of many cultures, and horse-drawn carriage rides through a glowing campus.

PHOTOS BY JIM HEEMSTRA

*Winter blankets Lagomarcino Hall (facing page), the Knoll (left) and central campus (below).*

JIM HEEMSTRA

*A snowy central campus as seen through the columns of Curtiss Hall.*

JIM HEEMSTRA

*A rain-soaked Lake LaVerne.*

JIM HEEMSTRA

ELIZABETH STANLEY

ISU PHOTO SERVICE

PHOTOS BY JIM HEEMSTRA

*Facing page, top: Spring surrounds Morrill Hall.*

*Facing page, bottom: A young couple near Lagomarcino Hall.*

*Above: Students in Lagomarcino Courtyard.*

*"Learning is always in season."*
– VIRGIL LAGOMARCINO

135

DON WISHART

*Below: Enjoying summer beneath the columns of Welch Hall.*

JIM HEEMSTRA

DON WISHART

JIM HEEMSTRA

JIM HEEMSTRA

JIM HEEMSTRA

ISU PHOTO SERVICE

JIM HEEMSTRA

JIM HEEMSTRA

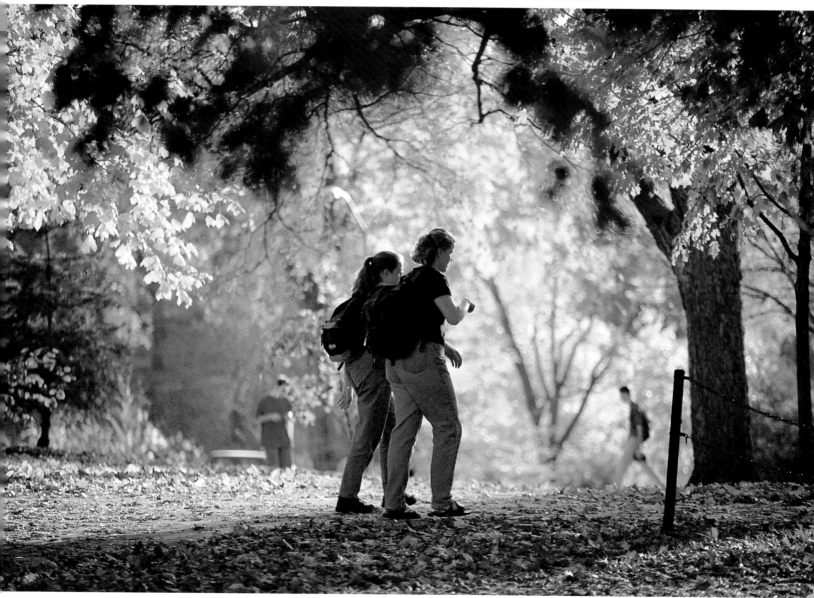

JIM HEEMSTRA

JIM HEEMSTRA

PETE KRUMHARDT

*"The third biennial meeting of the Alumni Association was held in the chapel in the evening of June 30th. Two or three days before the appointed time, the alumni began to arrive, and the familiarity with which they rushed up the stone steps to greet their delighted friends showed them to be no strangers to the institution. . . . It was gratifying to watch the happy expressions on their faces as they reviewed the trials they had endured, the victories they had achieved, and the pleasant hours they had enjoyed together during their college days."*

– RECALLING THE YEAR 1880,
FROM *HISTORY OF REMINISCES OF IOWA AGRICULTURAL COLLEGE*

For the first 46 years of its life, the Iowa State University Alumni Association was run totally by volunteers, and volunteers continue to be an integral part of the organization, particularly its Board of Directors. The first executive director arrived in 1893, and by the year 2000 the staff had grown to 18 members. Although the ISU Alumni Association has come a long way since that third meeting in 1880, its purpose remains constant: **To keep alumni connected.** The Association makes a lifetime connection with its alumni through its programs, services, and events.

## Programs, services, and events

The goal of the Alumni Association is to serve all alumni – and the organization also extends this goal to include future alumni – its current students. ISU students may belong to the Student Alumni Association, which introduces them to a lifetime of Association benefits, or they may become active in the Student Alumni Leadership Council, which organizes events such as Homecoming, Family Weekend, and Senior Class Council. Alumni of all ages stay connected to ISU through the Association's career services, professional coffees, ISU clubs, and more than 150 off-campus events throughout the country each year. As alumni begin their families, they may take advantage of the Association's

Legacy Program, which introduces their children to a future at ISU. The Association provides alumni with opportunities to give back to their alma mater through the Mentor Program for National Merit and Achievement Scholars, and the Going Places scholarship for students to study abroad.

The Association's Honors and Awards programs recognizes alumni, faculty, and staff with awards for outstanding service, for academic or professional achievements, and for having an impact on ISU's visibility.

Alumni can also stay connected with their ISU friends by using the Alumni Directory, online services, and through Class Notes in the *Iowa Stater*. The Association's quarterly magazine, VISIONS, brings alumni stories of ISU's people, trends, events, and issues.

## Alumni Association membership

More than 40,000 ISU alumni and friends make up the membership of the Alumni Association. Members enjoy access to the online Alumni Directory; they receive the electronic newsletter, *ISU News Flash*, and the award-winning calendar of university events. They also receive discounts on merchandise, services, and event fees. For more information on joining the Alumni Association, call toll-free 1-877-ISU-ALUM or visit the Association's Web site at www.isualum.org.